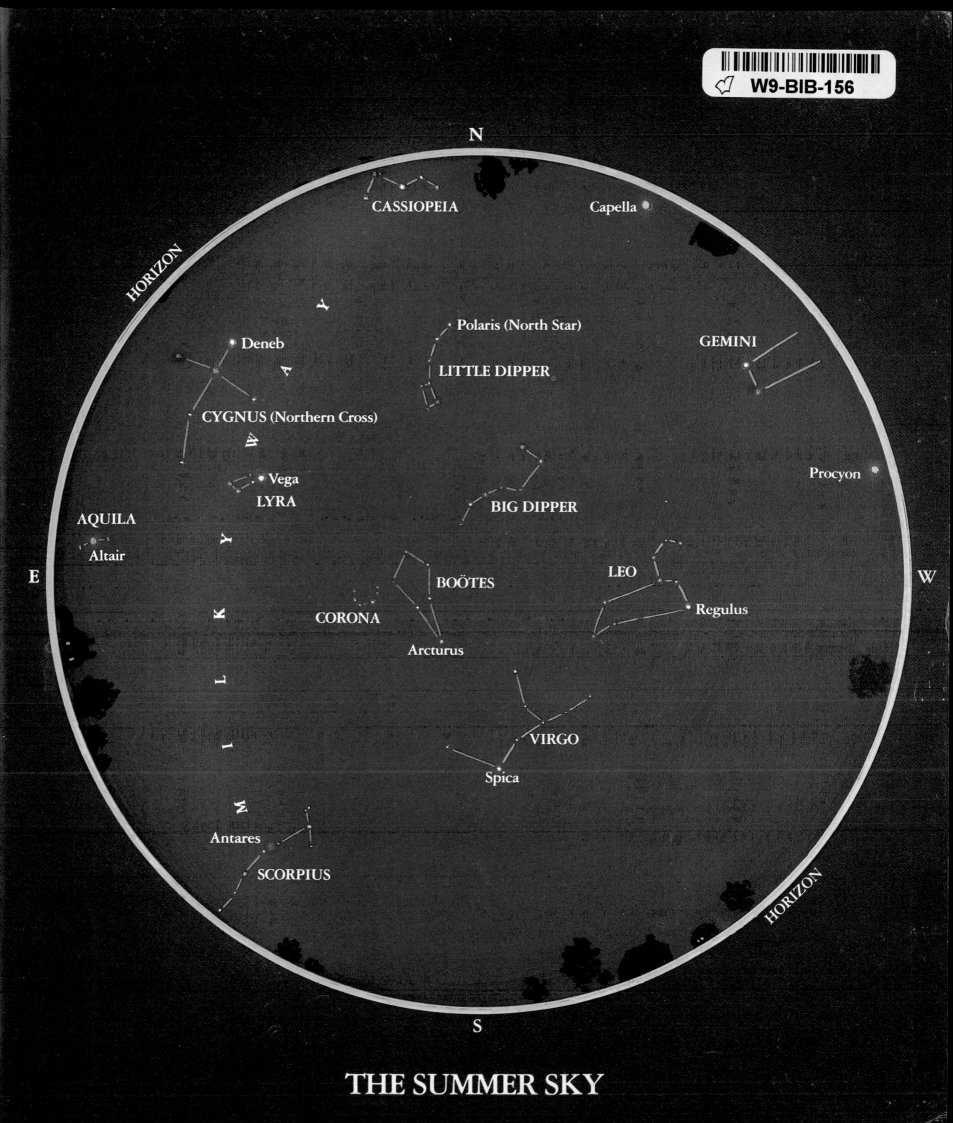

THE SUMMER SKY

Stars and Planets

Stars and

Planets

By Christopher Lampton
Illustrated by Ron Miller

Doubleday

The editor wishes to thank Lee Saegesser of NASA headquarters, for his careful review of the manuscript and illustrations for this book.

Art Direction by Diana Klemin
Designed by November and Lawrence, Inc.

Library of Congress Cataloging-in-Publication Data
Lampton, Christopher.
  Stars and planets.
  Summary: Examines the stars, planets, and smaller objects in the universe and discusses space exploration, unidentified flying objects, and our future in space.
  1. Stars—Juvenile literature. 2. Planets—Juvenile literature. 3. Astronomy—Juvenile literature. 4. Space sciences—Juvenile literature. [1. Stars. 2. Planets. 3. Astronomy. 4. Outer space—Exploration] I. Miller, Ron, 1947-   , ill. II. Title. III. Title: Stars and planets.
QB801.7.L36 1988   523   87–13628
ISBN 0-385-23785-5
ISBN 0-385-23786-3 (lib. bdg.)

First Edition

The Solar System

When you go outside on a dark, cloudless night, you can see one of the most beautiful sights in the universe just by looking up. You can see the stars.

People have been looking at the stars for thousands of years. Scientists called astronomers study the stars through special viewing instruments called telescopes.

The nearest star to Earth is the Sun. It is visible in the sky on a clear day, but you should never look at it directly. Direct sunlight can harm your eyes, even blind you.

The Sun is a star just like the ones that you see in the sky on a cloudless night. It looks so big and bright because it is a lot closer to us than any other star. Even so, the Sun is very far away. It is 93 million miles (149 million km) from Earth, which is farther than you'll travel in your lifetime. In fact, if you could drive to the Sun in a car, it would take you almost two hundred years to get there.

The Sun is big—almost a million miles across—and hot. The temperature at the surface of the Sun is 10,000 degrees Fahrenheit—twenty times hotter than the inside of your oven. The inside of the Sun is even hotter, up to 27,000,000 degrees Fahrenheit! If a spaceship fell into the Sun, it would burn up almost instantly.

You can feel the Sun's heat whenever you go outdoors. Even the coldest winter day would be colder still without the Sun. The Sun not only keeps us warm, it keeps us alive. Without it, none of Earth's living creatures—plants, animals, or humans—could possibly exist.

Pluto

Uranus

Mercury

Venus

Sun

Earth

Moving around the Sun are nine
planets. A planet is a large ball of rocky
or gaseous matter. You can see some of
these planets in the night sky, where
they look much like stars. They "shine"
by reflecting the light of the Sun.
Unlike the stars, the planets change
places in the sky from week to week
and month to month.

You can see one of these planets in
the daytime too. It is right beneath
your feet and it is called Earth. The
Earth is a ball of solid matter so big
that it would take you years to walk
around it, but it is still much, much
smaller than the Sun.

The Sun and the planets that move
around it are part of what we call the
solar system. Why do the planets move
around the Sun? The Sun produces a
powerful force called gravity that pulls
the planets toward it. In fact, every
object in the universe produces gravity.
It is the gravity produced by the Earth
that keeps you from falling off the
planet into outer space.

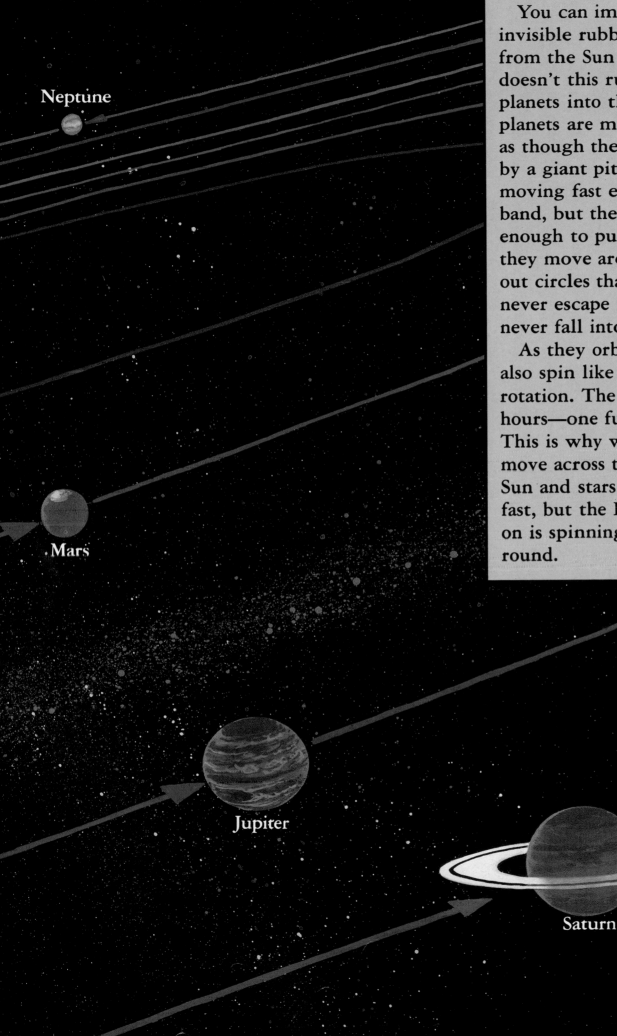

Neptune

Mars

Jupiter

Saturn

You can imagine gravity as a kind of invisible rubber band, reaching out from the Sun to each planet. Why doesn't this rubber band pull the planets into the Sun? Because the planets are moving at a very fast speed, as though they were baseballs thrown by a giant pitcher. They are not moving fast enough to break the rubber band, but the rubber band isn't strong enough to pull them into the Sun. So they move around the Sun in stretched-out circles that we call orbits. They never escape from the Sun, but they never fall into it either.

As they orbit the Sun, the planets also spin like tops. This spin is called rotation. The Earth takes twenty-four hours—one full day—for each rotation. This is why we see the Sun and stars move across the sky once a day. The Sun and stars are not really moving that fast, but the Earth that we are standing on is spinning like a giant merry-go-round.

The Inner Planets

The closest planet to the Sun is Mercury. It is also the second smallest planet in the solar system. Up close, Mercury looks a lot like the Moon, covered with holes called craters. These holes were dug by large rocks that struck Mercury and other planets very early in the life of the solar system.

There are great soaring cliffs on the surface of Mercury, called scarps. These cliffs probably appeared because the planet shrunk after it was born—the same reason that wrinkles form on prunes and raisins!

A day on Mercury is equal to fifty-eight Earth days, because that's how long it takes for the planet to rotate only once. But a year on Mercury—or the time needed to complete its orbit around the Sun—is only eighty-eight Earth days long. That's much less than an Earth year and less than two Mercury days!

Although Mercury is the closest planet to the Sun, it is not the hottest. Venus, the second planet from the Sun, is even hotter—900 degrees Fahrenheit on the surface. Why is it so hot? Because the planet is wrapped in thick clouds of gas called carbon dioxide, which trap the Sun's heat like the windows of a greenhouse. When we look at Venus, we are seeing the tops of these clouds. We cannot see the surface of Venus, even with a telescope, but we can "see" it with radar, the way that air traffic controllers "see" airplanes. We can see, for instance, that there are two giant plateaus on Venus that we call Ishtar Terra and Aphrodite Terra. Like Venus itself, they are both named after mythical goddesses. (The word Terra means "land.") Most of the surface of Venus, though, is covered with rolling plains.

A day on Venus is 117 Earth days long, even longer than a day on Mercury. Venus orbits the Sun once every 225 days.

Sunrise over a cliff (scarp) on Mercury

Typical scene on Venus

Venus

The third planet from the Sun is Earth, the planet that we live on. The Earth is larger than either Venus or Mercury, and is the only planet in the solar system that human beings can live on without spacesuits or special houses. As far as we know, it is the only planet that *anything* lives on.

Earth is also the only planet that has the large bodies of water that we call oceans. Seen from space, the Earth is a beautiful ball of colors—blue oceans, white clouds, and brown continents.

In recent years, scientists have learned that the surface of the Earth is made up of several large "plates," which float about on the Earth's mantle, the semi-liquid substance that lies a few miles below the planet's crust. The continents of Earth—North and South America, Africa, Europe, Asia, Australia, and Antarctica—are part of these plates. The plates do not move quickly, but millions of years ago the surface of the Earth looked quite different than it looks today. All of the continents were bunched together into one big supercontinent that scientists call Pangaea, from Greek words meaning "all the Earth."

Mars, the fourth planet, is smaller than the Earth. Once, it was believed that there might be living creatures on Mars. But when two spacecraft, Viking I and Viking II, landed on Mars in 1976, they found no evidence of life.

Earth's Moon

Earth

Mars is a barren desert. It is covered with red dust, which is why we call Mars the "red planet."

The air on Mars is thin—and cold. In the summer, the temperature can go as high as 70 degrees, but on a winter night it is colder than anywhere on Earth. Once or twice a year, giant dust storms sweep across the surface of Mars, blotting out everything but the highest mountains.

There is almost no water on the surface of Mars, but there are winding, streamlike canyons that look like they were carved long ago by flooding water. Where did this water go? No one knows, but it may be deep inside the planet.

The most impressive feature on Mars is a giant volcano called Olympus Mons ("Mount Olympus"). Olympus Mons, which may be the largest mountain in the solar system, is more than 15 miles (25 km) high. It is part of a group of volcanoes in the region of Mars called Tharsis Ridge.

Mercury, Venus, Earth, and Mars are called the inner planets, because they are the closest to the Sun. The next four planets, called the gas giants, are very different from the inner planets. The inner planets are small and rocky. The gas giants are large and icy. One of the gas giants, Jupiter, is larger than all of the other planets put together.

A typical landscape on Mars

The Outer Planets

Jupiter is the fifth planet from the Sun. It is named after the greatest of the Roman gods and for good reason. It would take more than a thousand Earths to equal one Jupiter.

Jupiter is surprisingly hot—but much of this heat comes from *inside* the planet instead of from the Sun. This heat stirs up giant storms in the clouds that surround the planet. One of these storms is a hurricane bigger than Earth. We call this storm the Great Red Spot, because of the way it looks through a telescope. This storm has been raging for at least three hundred years.

Jupiter may not have a "surface" the way that the inner planets do. When we look at Jupiter through a telescope, we see only the colored tops of its clouds, painting huge stripes across the planet.

The sixth planet, Saturn, is the most beautiful in the solar system. Circling this planet are a set of giant rings made out of tiny chunks of ice, dust, and rock. (Jupiter also has rings, made out of tiny rocklike particles, but they are hard to see and not very pretty.) When the famous Italian astronomer Galileo first saw these rings through a small telescope, in 1610, he thought that they were "handles" attached to the sides of the planet. Although these rings are hundreds of thousands of miles across, they are less than a mile thick. When they tilt so that their edges are facing earth (as they do every fifteen years or so) the rings almost seem to disappear.

Saturn is the second largest planet in the solar system. Like Jupiter, much of the planet is made of ice and gas. Unlike

Jupiter

Earth scaled to size in comparison to the "gas giar

Uranus

Saturn

Neptune

Jupiter, Saturn may have a solid core made out of iron at the center of this ice and gas. This core is probably about the size of Earth.

Beyond Saturn is Uranus, the seventh planet. In 1986 a spaceship called Voyager passed close to Uranus and returned the first close-up pictures of this planet to scientists on Earth. In a few days we learned more about Uranus than astronomers had learned in two and a half centuries of watching it through telescopes.

Uranus is big and gives off a greenish glow. It too has rings like Saturn and Jupiter. Although it is much bigger than the Earth, it would still take twenty planets the size of Uranus to equal one Jupiter.

The strange thing about Uranus is that it spins on its side. If all of the planets in the solar system are spinning tops, the Uranus top must have fallen over. It may have been knocked over by a wandering planet billions of years ago.

The last of the gas giants is Neptune. Little is known about Neptune because it is so far away. It is thirty times farther from the Sun than the Earth is. Neptune may be the only gas giant without rings, though it is too far away for us to know for sure.

Neptune was discovered in 1846, after two scientists had predicted its position in the sky based on the effect its gravity was having on Uranus. The temperature on Neptune's surface is 220 degrees below zero, Centigrade. This is very cold, but not as cold as scientists think it should be, given its distance from the Sun. Probably, some of the heat comes from inside the planet, just as some of Jupiter's heat comes from inside Jupiter.

There is one more planet in the solar system and it isn't a gas giant. Pluto is the smallest of all the planets, only about twice as big as the Moon. It is always night on Pluto. From Pluto, the Sun looks like just another star in the sky.

Neptune

Surface of Neptune's moon, Triton

The Sun

Pluto

Usually, we call Neptune the eighth planet of the solar system and Pluto the ninth. But Pluto has a lopsided orbit around the Sun. In the late 1970s, it moved closer to the Sun than Neptune. Pluto is now the eighth planet and Neptune is the ninth. In the year 1999, Pluto will become the ninth planet once again.

Whatever its place in the solar system, Pluto was indeed the last of the nine planets to be discovered and the only one discovered in this century, in 1930. And besides being the smallest of the planets it's also the coldest, with a surface temperature of 230 degrees below zero, Centigrade. In fact, some scientists believe that the planet may be a solid ball of ice.

There is more to the solar system than just the Sun and the planets. The solar system contains lesser objects as well— and some of these "lesser" objects are larger than some of the planets.

Pluto's moon, Charon

Moons

The solar system can be considered our "neighborhood" in space. Alas, it is not as easy for us to visit our neighbors in space as it is for you to visit the neighbors on your block. In fact, we have only visited one of our solar neighbors, the closest of them all—the Moon.

Just as the planets move around the Sun in their orbits, the Moon moves around the Earth. The Earth's gravity keeps the Moon from drifting into space, just as the Sun's gravity keeps the planets from escaping.

The Moon is 240,000 miles (385,000 km) from the Earth's surface. It travels around the Earth in a little less than twenty-eight days, moving into a different part of the sky every night.

Like the planets, the Moon seems to shine because it reflects the light of the Sun. When we look at the Moon from Earth, the part that the Sun is shining on looks light and the rest looks dark. That's because the Sun only shines on half of the Moon at one time.

Earth's Moon

← Apollo 11 landing site

Typical scene on the Moon

The Moon also spins, like a planet. It takes the Moon a little less than twenty-eight days to spin once—exactly the same time it takes the Moon to go around the Earth. This is why the same side of the Moon is always facing toward Earth. To see the other side, we must send rockets around the Moon to take pictures.

The Moon is very large. In diameter, it is one fourth as big as the Earth. Scientists have trouble explaining how such a large object came to be revolving around the Earth. The best guess is that billions of years ago another large object, about the size of the Moon, crashed into the Earth. This collision sent pieces of hot rock flying into orbit around the Earth. Some of these pieces of rock came from the large object that hit the Earth, but most of them came from the Earth itself. As these pieces of rock bumped into one another and cooled, they formed the Moon.

Through a telescope, we can see that the Moon is covered with large holes called craters. Most of these craters, like the ones on Mercury, were created billions of years ago, when large rocks crashed into the Moon, leaving behind a thick layer of dust covering the Moon's surface. There are also dark areas on the Moon that look like oceans. They are called maria, from a Latin word meaning "seas." There is no water in these seas, though. They are filled with lava from the eruptions of volcanoes. These eruptions also took place billions of years ago. There are no more live volcanoes on the Moon.

The Earth is not the only planet that has a moon circling around it. In fact, all of the other planets, except for Mercury and Venus, have moons. Most have more than one.

Mars has two moons, called Phobos and Deimos. They are very small, but they are also much closer to the surface of Mars than Earth's Moon is to its surface. Phobos is only 5,800 miles (9,300 km) away from Mars.

Jupiter has at least sixteen moons—and maybe more that we don't know about. The four biggest moons are called the Galilean moons, because they were first seen nearly four hundred years ago by the astronomer Galileo Galilei. Each Galilean moon is like a planet in its own right. One of them, Ganymede, is larger than either Pluto or Mercury.

Just as Jupiter is the largest planet, so Ganymede is the largest moon in the solar system. In photographs, Ganymede looks a lot like Earth's Moon, but its surface is covered with ice. Callisto, the second largest of Jupiter's moons, is also covered with ice, as is Europa, the smallest. Astronomers think that the cracked ice on Europa's surface may hide a giant ocean. Io, the third largest moon,

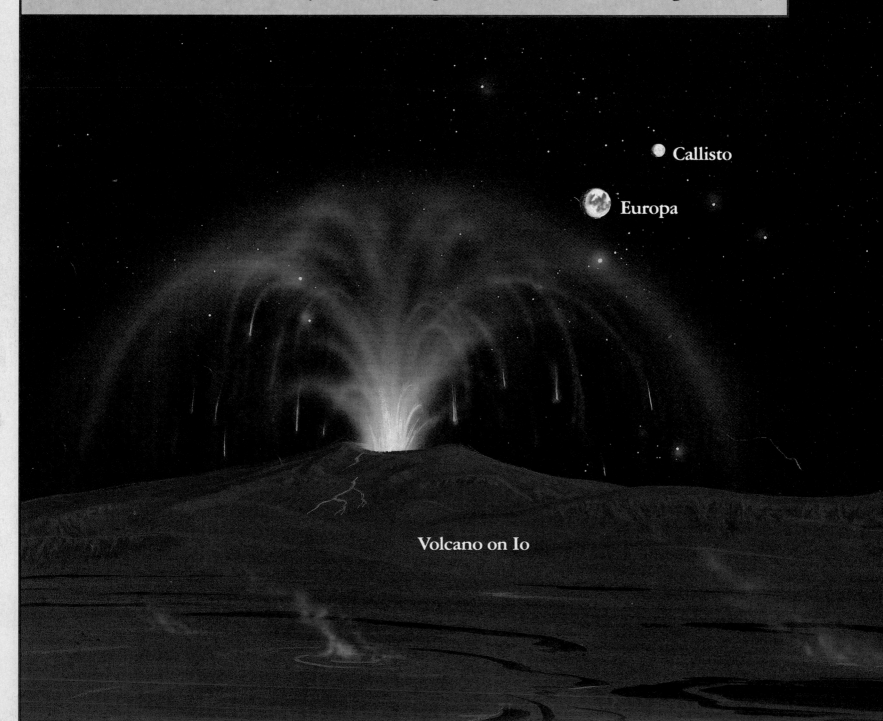

Callisto

Europa

Volcano on Io

has a hot surface covered with volcanoes, some of which are still active.

Saturn has at least twenty-two moons. The largest, Titan, is a lot like a planet. Some astronomers think Titan looks like the Earth did billions of years ago. The other large moons—Mimas, Enceladus, Tethys, Iapetus, Dione, and Rhea—are more like Earth's Moon. Mimas has a large crater on one side that looks like a giant eye.

Uranus has fifteen moons that we know about. The five largest moons are named Miranda, Ariel, Umbriel, Titania, and Oberon. All except Umbriel show

signs of past volcanic activity. Miranda's surface is covered with the strangest landscape in the solar system: soaring cliffs, dark circles, deep valleys, and very old craters.

Neptune has only two known moons. Named Triton and Nereid, they both behave in strange ways. Scientists think that the orbit of Triton is slowing down —and that the moon will eventually fall into Neptune. Nereid has a lopsided orbit that is not like any other moon in the solar system.

Even tiny Pluto has a moon—Charon— almost half as big as Pluto itself.

Miranda

Uranus

The surface of Ariel

Asteroids

Moons aren't the only things in the solar system besides planets. Between the orbits of Mars and Jupiter are a number of small objects called asteroids. The word "asteroid" means starlike, but the asteroids are more planetlike than starlike. Sometimes they are called minor planets. Like planets, they revolve around the Sun and shine in its reflected light.

The largest asteroid is Ceres. It is 620 miles (1,000 km) across. Not many other asteroids are this big, but thousands of them are larger than a mile across. Some are no bigger than boulders. There must be trillions of asteroids in all, most of them too small to see through a telescope. Where did these asteroids come from? An astronomer once suggested that they are the remains of a planet that fell apart. This probably isn't true, though they may be the pieces of a planet that was about to form, but never did.

Not all asteroids orbit the Sun between Mars and Jupiter. Some asteroids wander closer to the Sun, sometimes passing near the Earth. These are called Earth-crossers, or Apollo asteroids. (Apollo was the name of the first Earth-crosser ever discovered.) In the past, some of these asteroids may have collided with the Earth. Such an asteroid collision would have been harmful to living creatures on this planet. Dust thrown into the air by an asteroid would black out the Sun. The weather would be very cold for years afterward. Many scientists believe this may be what killed the dinosaurs, 65 million years ago. Asteroid collisions are very rare, though, and it's unlikely that one will occur in the near future.

Asteroids

The Life of a Star

We saw in the last chapter how a star is born. After it is born, it grows up, grows old . . . and dies. Some stars die quiet deaths. But others die violently, in huge explosions. And what happens to a star after it is dead is often more interesting than what happens while it is alive.

Hydrogen fusion can keep a star hot for a long time, but sooner or later a star uses up its hydrogen atoms and runs out of fuel. This will happen to our Sun in five billion years. When it runs out of fuel, it will start shrinking again, just like the hydrogen cloud from which it was born.

As it shrinks, it will heat up, just as the original protostar heated up as its atoms collided. Our sun will turn red in color and inflate like a balloon. It may swallow up the inner planets, including the Earth. Such a giant red star is called a red giant. We can see other red giants through telescopes. The most famous is the star named Betelgeuse. Betelgeuse is a *big* star, about 800 million miles across.

Surface of Red Giant

White Dwarf (orbiting Red Giant)

After another billion years, our Sun will start shrinking again. It will keep shrinking until it becomes so small that it can't shrink any more. The atoms in the sun—some of them, at least—will be squeezed into a tight ball of atoms called a white dwarf. The rest will escape into space in a cloud of gas and dust called a planetary nebula.

The white dwarf will be small, about the size of the Earth. The atoms in the white dwarf will be packed together so tightly that a teaspoon of white dwarf matter would weigh a ton. Like a star, the white dwarf will keep glowing for billions of years. Then it will cool off and become a black dwarf.

Supernovas

Supernova

This is the way that some stars die, but not very large stars. A large star grows so hot at the end of its life that it explodes. This explosion is called a supernova. For a few days, the exploding star produces as much light and heat as an entire galaxy of stars.

In February 1987, astronomers in South America discovered a supernova explosion in the Large Magellanic Cloud, a small galaxy not far from the Milky Way. The explosion, which was visible to the naked eye for several weeks, was the closest supernova that astronomers have observed in nearly four hundred years, since before the invention of the telescope. The actual explosion took place about 170,000 years ago, but the light from the explosion has only now reached Earth, having traveled across many thousands of light-years of space. This supernova will tell us important things about the way that stars die.

When a large star explodes, most of its atoms are blown away into space. But the matter at the center of the star is squeezed into a very tiny ball by the explosion. The atoms in this ball are crushed and knocked apart into smaller particles called neutrons. (Neutrons are one of the particles from which atoms are "built.") This ball of neutrons is called a neutron star. A neutron star is much smaller than a white dwarf—about ten miles across!

Black Holes

When a *very* big star dies, it explodes with such force that even the neutrons in the neutron star are crushed. All of the matter in the center of the star is squeezed into a tiny area of space, much the way our universe may have been before the big bang. This tiny point of crushed matter produces so much gravity that not even light can get away from it. The star becomes invisible. Nothing that comes close to the star can ever escape. We call such a star a black hole.

We can't see black holes through telescopes because they are invisible. But a black hole would have lots of hot matter around it, attracted by its gravity. This matter would become hot because the atoms in the matter would bump together, like the atoms in a protostar. Then it would swirl around the black hole in a giant whirlpool before it fell in. This whirlpool would produce a special kind of light called X rays.

Astronomers use X-ray telescopes orbiting around the Earth to look for black holes. They have found several sources of X rays that may be black holes.

Even other stars can fall into a black hole. At the center of a galaxy, stars are closer together than at the outer edges. If a black hole formed there, it might swallow all of the nearby stars and grow very large. As it grew larger, it would swallow still more stars. Because it would be so large, it would attract an unusually large—and hot—whirlpool of matter around it. In fact, the matter around the black hole might become so hot that it would produce explosions much larger than the supernova that created the black hole.

Could there be a black hole in the center of our own galaxy? We can't see what is happening there because of the dark clouds in the way. But radio waves from the center of our galaxy tell us that something strange is going on there. These radio waves may be produced by a giant black hole swallowing nearby stars.

A Black Hole can swallow entire stars through the force of its gravity.

Exploring the Universe

Astronomers have been watching the skies for thousands of years. For most of that time, they had their eyes alone with which to study the stars. Then, in 1610, the telescope was invented. Just as the lenses in eyeglasses help people to see better, the lenses in a telescope help us view the universe more clearly. A telescope makes stars look closer, so that astronomers can study them in more detail.

The most exciting advance in astronomy in this century is the space probe. Not only can we study objects in space with telescopes, we can actually go to those objects and look at them up close. The first space probes were launched in the early 1960s, to Mars, Venus, and the Moon. In 1976, the Viking space probe landed on the planet Mars and returned photographs of its surface.

The two Voyager space probes, launched in 1977, returned beautiful color photographs of Jupiter, Saturn, Uranus, and their moons. In 1989, one of the Voyager probes will return photographs of the planet Neptune.

We can even send human beings into outer space, where they can collect samples from other worlds and return with them. So far, however, no human being has gone farther than the Moon. In the years 1969 through 1972, spaceships carried twelve astronauts to the Moon. They returned with cargoes of Moon rocks for scientists on Earth to examine.

Space shuttle

Space observatory

35

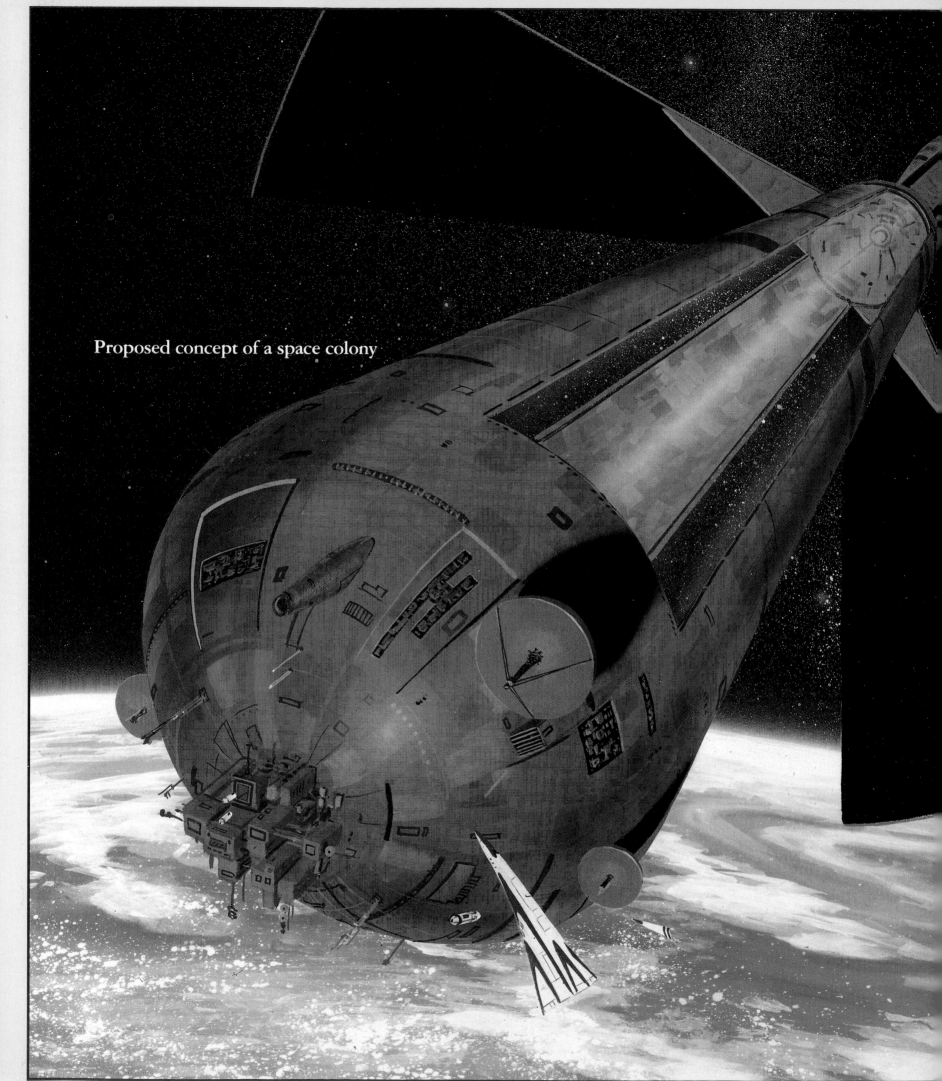

Proposed concept of a space colony

Today, astronauts in the United States travel to space in space shuttles, which are part rocket and part airplane. Americans were deeply saddened when a space shuttle accidentally exploded in 1986, killing seven astronauts. The American space program was temporarily suspended after this tragic accident.

When the space program is revived, the United States is scheduled to build a space station in orbit around the Earth, sometime in the 1990s. Astronauts will live for months on board this station, performing experiments.

If people are going to work in space, they will need to live in space as well, and not just for a few months at a time. Giant space colonies will be built that contain entire cities, in orbit around the Earth. People will live their entire lives inside these colonies. Perhaps someday one of these colonies, equipped with rockets, will leave Earth orbit and take off to explore the stars.

The stars are a long way off and it will take a long time to get there. The rockets that we use to explore space today would take many thousands of years to reach the nearest star. But just as we are now beginning to explore the Moon and the planets, human beings will someday want to explore the stars.

When we get there, what will we find? Strange new solar systems? Surprising new stars?

And maybe something—or someone—else?

Mirrors to reflect sunlight inside

Typical scene inside proposed space colony

Many scientists believe that life began in the ocean.

Is Anybody There?

When we reach the stars, will there be anyone waiting for us? Or are we the only intelligent creatures in the universe? For that matter, are we the only living things in the universe?

We are probably the only living things in the solar system. Mercury and Venus are too hot for life. Mars is too cold. Life might exist in the hot clouds of Jupiter, but it isn't very likely. There might be something alive on Titan, the largest moon of Saturn, but it won't be intelligent. The other planets are too cold, too far away from the sun.

There may be planets revolving around other stars, and a few of them may be like Earth. If we ever get to these planets, we may find plants and animals. We may even find intelligent beings, like us.

Some scientists believe that life is very common throughout this galaxy, and in other galaxies. Others believe that it is rare. A few think that human beings are the only intelligent living things in the universe.

To figure out if there could be life on other worlds, we must understand why there is life on Earth. The first living things appeared on Earth about four billion years ago. This is a long time, and it's hard to say exactly how those living things got here. Most scientists believe that life began in the ocean.

According to this theory, the ocean of four billion years ago was full of chemicals. These chemicals were made up of atoms, linked together to form long chains called molecules. Many, many different kinds of molecules formed in the early ocean. Some were very much like the molecules that are found in living creatures. By accident, a molecule formed that could make copies of itself. The copies of this molecule could also make copies of themselves. And some of them did this better than the originals!

In time, some of these molecules grouped together to form collections of molecules called organisms. Over billions of years, these organisms grew larger and more complicated. Every living creature on earth today is a descendant of these early organisms.

If the Earth had been a little closer to the Sun, it would have been too hot for these living molecules to form. If it had been a little farther away, it would have been too cold. If the Earth had been smaller, it wouldn't have enough gravity to hold on to an atmosphere, so there would have been nothing for the living molecules to breathe. There might not be many planets where the conditions for life are as perfect as on Earth.

If there *are* intelligent beings living on planets orbiting other stars, why haven't they built spaceships and visited us? Some people think they have. People have been seeing unidentified flying objects, or UFOs, for hundreds of years. Most of these, however, have turned out to be such "ordinary" things as clouds, airplanes, satellites, even the planet Venus. There is no evidence that any UFO was really a spaceship from another planet.

If intelligent beings *haven't* visited us, as most scientists believe, it may mean that they do not exist. Or maybe it is so difficult to travel between stars that no intelligent race of beings has ever tried it. Or maybe they just haven't found us yet.

Even if we never meet other intelligent beings face to face, we still may be able to talk with them by radio. Radio waves can travel vast distances. Radio travels at the speed of light, but even light takes four years to reach the nearest star. A short radio conversation with beings in another solar system would take many years, maybe even centuries. But it would surely be one of the most interesting and important conversations in human history.

Index

About the Author

An "amateur astronomer" since youth, Christopher Lampton turned his love of stargazing into a career and has written nearly thirty books on science subjects for children and young adults.

The author was born in Texas and raised in the Washington, D.C., area. After graduation from the University of Maryland in 1973, he pursued a career in broadcasting. He later turned to writing full time and has been doing so for over ten years from his home in Maryland.

About the Artist

Born and raised in the Midwest, Ron Miller has illustrated many books and national magazine articles on astronomy. A graduate of the Columbus (Ohio) College of Art and Design, he worked for several commercial art studios before joining the Smithsonian's National Air and Space Museum as art director for the Albert Einstein Planetarium. He left the museum to open his own art studio, from which he produces mainly astronomical and science fiction artwork. Mr. Miller is a founding member of the International Association of Astronomical Artists, a member of NASA's Fine Arts Program, and a contributor to the National Commission on Space and NASA's Solar System Exploration Committee.

He lives in Virginia with his wife, Judith, and five cats.

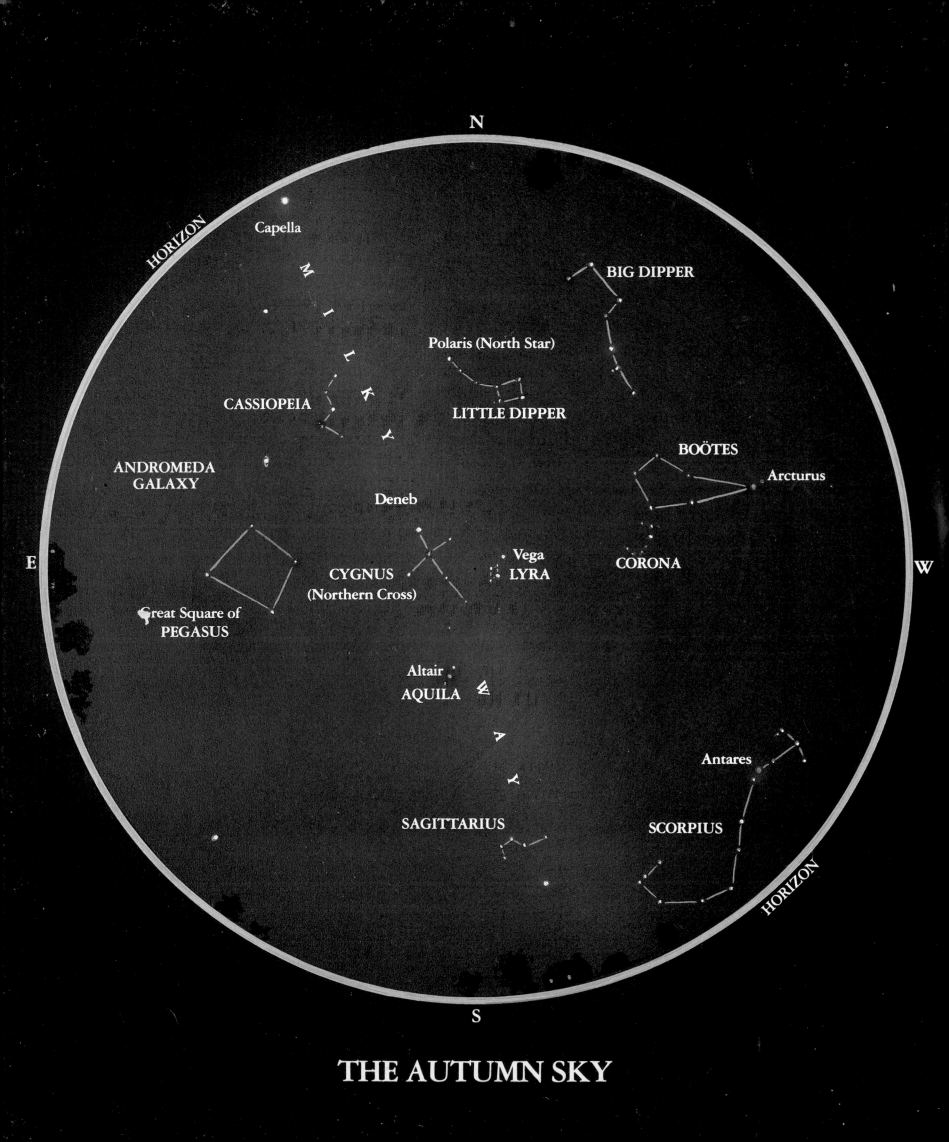

THE AUTUMN SKY